Steps to Free Yourself from Child Support

Stop Giving Your Energy Away

Author: Devion Glass

Quote

If you don't know the answer to the situation your facing. Look within then you shall find the keys to set yourself truly free.

—ELSHAADDI

Dedication & Loving Memory

to My Mother
Pamela (The Goddess) Glass
My Brothers King Sia & King Blacc

Steps to Free Yourself from Child Support Copyright © 2017 by Devion Glass. All Rights Reserved.

All rights reserved. No part of this book may be reproduced in any form or by any electronic or mechanical means including information storage and retrieval systems, without permission in writing from the author. The only exception is by a reviewer, who may quote short excerpts in a review.

Cover designed by Devion Glass

This book is a work of non-fiction. Any resemblance to actual persons, living or dead, events, or locales is entirely true.

Devion Glass
Google the name EL Shaaddi

Printed in the United States of America

First Printing: Mar 2019
Arq Angelz Entertainment LLC.

ISBN-9781091057241

Stop Giving Your Energy Away

Preface

Hello, my name is Devion Glass. I am a young man who experienced this issue first and second hand. I was born and raised in the heart of Saint Louis, Missouri. Raised in a single parented household with his mother and siblings. Knowledge and the streets were the outlets from the pain that I faced growing up. I grew up in the system by the age of 8. Long story my life has its ups and downs like everyone else. The reason for me writing this e-book is because of my personal problems in life with my daughter's mother.

I started doing research once I started receiving paperwork from my job about being put on child support. Also, them taking deductions out of my pay check. I had to go to their office and request the information that was supposed to be mailed to me. It never was. The address they had on file wasn't mines. Nobody stayed at that resident for months. So, with these so-called powers they implemented an administrative order. Without my consent. The so-called debit I never accepted.

Stop Giving Your Energy Away

So, me being a thinker that's not right. Is what I stated to self. Come to find out the whole corporate entity is a fraud. I have proof. I am not going to go any further with my story. Here's how my journey into freeing myself began.

Contents

Steps to Free Yourself from Child Support 1
Quote 2
Dedication & Loving Memory 3
Preface 5
Contents 7
Chapter 1: 8
The Breakdown 8
Chapter 2: 13
Case Files 13
Chapter 3: 17
The Master Plan 17
Glossary 24
References 27
Stop Giving Your Energy Away INC 30

Chapter 1: The Breakdown

What is child support? Now that is a great question to ask. The average person think that this is law. In all actuality it is not law but a provision. This entity that is calling itself Child Support started as part of the executive branch of the federal government. It started from The Social Security Act of 1935.

"3125.01 Title IV-D case defined. As used in the chapter, "Title IV-D case" means any case in which the child support enforcement agency is enforcing the child support order pursuant to Title IV-D of the "Social Security Act," 88 Stat. 2351 (1975), 42 U.S.C. 651, as amended."

Now this might get a little serious because now there are only three ways to get put on child support. First, child support is voluntary

Second, Paternity has to be established on parent who they are trying to have pay this debit. Third, the birth certificate, marriage license, and DNA are the only way you can get put on child support. Majority of the people who get put on child support title-IV are labeled as a dead-beat parent. I know this for a fact because I've been in my child life been taking care of her before she was born a once, she came. Just because her mother wanted help or something like that. They thought I was going to pay for their help.

Who owns this entity?

The child support system that we know of is a branch from the executive federal government. This comes from the Social Security Act of 1935 which was never passed as law. The law is that all three powers stay separate so there is now way that should be able to go to jail from this. Well once you signed the contract you accepted the consequences they say. In the process of trying to hide the truth they commit fraud.

The federal government pays the state for the money that they can get from the parent on child support. In so many words the estates taking you money to get funding from the federal level. Now you night be asking yourself. How is this possible? Where did they violate my rights? What are the real dealings with the birth certificate, marriage license, and the DNA testing? So many thoughts went through my head once I found out that I basically signed my daughter over to the state and that is why child support was being issued on me. To go a further into this entity. Like I stated early that this entity is a fraudulent system to get your money.

How is child support title-IV a fraud?

Ask yourself this did you know that these documents are considered contracts whether it says agreement or contract. Remember this in law an agreement is a contract. They are the same thing stated in different forms. The rights you have are the entitlement to due process of law. They have to verbally or have written down the consequences of you signing this contract in full detail. Now, if you need that once you signed the birth certificate that you could be put on child support, have your wages garnished, driver's license revoked and so much more. No, you didn't.

    Logic and truth always will make you think. The supreme court in different cases has ruled this provision child support isn't law. it doesn't truly

Stop Giving Your Energy Away

support our children. I'm not going to get into much on all of the cases because that's the next chapter. As well as breaking down the contracts with the birth certificate, marriage license, and the DNA is in another book that I'm writing so be on the lookout for that. Not to stir away from the main topic of the book but this knowledge goes for man or woman. It's not about race or color in this aspect of life.

I have friends and family members who are being raped of their funds to benefit the bank account of the elites. If the system was never set up for you to fail you wouldn't. The contracts that are in place with this corporate entity are with-in the state, cities, and counties. These agreements with the state allow them to send out arrest warrants etc.

These things affect everyday life for people. You wonder why it's so hard to succeed.

From This!!

https://www.jimsjourney.org/hannibal-slavery/

To This

https://www.southerncoalition.org/mass-incarceration-people-color/

Stop Giving Your Energy Away

Chapter 2: Case Files

There is a better understanding of this subject that is being discussed feelings can't be involved. There are a lot of cases that make this corporate entity is a fraud. Most people might call me crazy for doing this. Why you not supporting your child? It's nothing like that I promise you. I take care of my child always has and always will. You don't need to be threaten or thrown in jail for not being able to. Now in some cases this is needed and here's why. Some people lives are being destroyed from child support because of the other parent. When normally it's their fault. Here are some cases that explains this fraudulent corporation. The first thing to know is about the case Mason v. Bradley, 789 F. Supp. 273 (N.D. Ill. 1992) US

District Court for the Northern District of Illinois - 789 F. Supp. 273 (N.D. Ill. 1992) "

Illinois, like other states which have voluntarily agreed to participate in the A.F.D.C program, are required to offer child support services as a condition of federal funding. The implementing regulations 277 provide some specific time frames for the states to follow, such as the 75-day period in which efforts to locate absent parents must be made after such efforts are deemed necessary."

Another case that is needed to be known is the case of Blessing v. Freestone, 520 U.S. 329 (1997). This case was really interesting to me. the reason for that is it deals with five Arizona mothers whose children are eligible for state child support services under Title IV -D of the Social Security Act, filed this 42 U. S. C. § 1983. A suit against petitioner, the director of the state child support agency. In so many words this case can get deep. There are several more cases that are going to be elaborated over. I'm not going to go into depth on everyone Check the back of the book. Last case that

I am going to discuss is child support system is declared unconstitutional. It deals with the case

STATE OF MINNESOTA

IN COURT OF APPEALS C7-97-926 C8-97-1132 C7-97-1512 C8-98-33, Filed

June 12, 1998. Now this case is funny to me because the state filed this against the agency. here's what it says and I quote, " "The administrative child support process created by Minn. Stat.

518.5511 (1996) violates the separation of powers doctrine by infringing on the district court's original jurisdiction, by creating a tribunal which is not inferior to the district court, and by permitting child support officers to practice law. Therefore, the statute is unconstitutional." So, you can see this whole operation that is going on totally is a fraud. These three cases plus a couple more are what I used to free myself. You have to prove that its fraud. The evidence I've presented will state that. For a better understanding there is one thing that will make sure you are all set.

Joy D. WEHUNT, Plaintiff, v. James G. LEDBETTER, in his official capacity as

Commissioner of the Georgia Department of Human Resources and Louis Sullivan, Defendants-Appellees.

Gwendolyn Brown, Intervenor-Appellant.

45 CFR § 302.34 – Cooperative arrangements. Such arrangements shall contain provisions for providing courts and law enforcement officials with pertinent information needed in locating noncustodial parents, establishing paternity and securing support, to the extent that such information is relevant to the duties to be performed pursuant to the arrangement. They shall also provide for assistance to the IV-D agency in carrying out the program, and may relate to any other matters of common concern. Under matters of common concern, such arrangements may include provisions for the investigation and prosecution of fraud directly related to paternity and child and spousal support, and provisions to reimburse courts and law enforcement officials for their assistance. These are a couple of more case that will help support the fraud under due process.

Stop Giving Your Energy Away

It's really up to you how. These cases are meant to be studied and remembered.

Chapter 3: The Master Plan

The next thing that is recommend for you to do is study the case. Once you do that you will understand the contracts that are set up with the federal and state government for Title-IV. Which makes the federal government have separate contracts with the municipals with your city/state.

After all the money is going to the state Treasury. Why would I say that is your judges get paid from that first before every other official/representative of the United States Corporation in your state. So, it's in the best interest of the overseer for the state to keep you on child support. The get funding from the federal government. So, you can sue the "judges" as well.

Another thing I suggest is that you do not go in these courts stating you are a color or a brand such as African American, Black, Negro, Indian just to name a few. Learn and study The Black Codes of

1724 & 1868. If you want to sue go get a JS44 form your city hall. The law knows you by nationality not brands. So, you will be immediately be looked at like your illiterate. Understand this whether we like it or not majority of the people on child support are melanin (Black) men. Whites are only on child support because of default. I'm not calling us black that doesn't make sense.

The law and the rest of the world knows as Aboriginals/Moors/Ebrews/Egyptians decedents.

Who were already over here? I'm getting to far ahead and off subject but look at it like this. If you ancestors where from Africa. Why haven't all the melanin men in prison been deported yet.

The answer is common sense you are not from there. You have direct ties to that land but your bloodline is from the continents North, Central, and South Americas. Well Thank you for your time out of your busy day to read this bit of information I will show you how I set up my letter that I used for my prom at hand.

Devion Glass Notice for Removal of Contract

This is a notice that I have never received a fair trial on this case. I never received the paperwork that I was supposed to have been served. I got a piece of mail from my place of employment talking about with-holding of a certain amount of funds. I went to the Wainwright Building Ste. 204 to get the information on February 7, 2019. So, an administrative order to push it through without my consent on contestant of the situation was issue. The sheriff gave a false statement. He stated that he served me at the address 4526 Alice Ave St. Louis, Missouri on 11/06/2018.

First, of that is a lie because I have no association to that house. That house was vacant since September 27, 2018. My friend mother stayed there and when helped him move her to Nebraska on9/27/2018. He also stated that he didn't serve me, but he gave the paperwork to my brother. Which also is a lie. My brother stays in Belleville and receives his paperwork about child support to

Stop Giving Your Energy Away

the Illinois address above. On 11/06/2018 my brother was at work in Belleville. If he served my brother, I need the paperwork stating my brother signed for this specific documentation. Which is a lie. You will not fine my brother signature on any documents with my name on it or him accepting the paperwork from the sheriff. I also, have voice recording of me entering that day and of the representative stating what the sheriff wrote.

Title IV-D of the Social Security Act, 42 U.S.C.A. 651 to -669b this act isn't law it is a provision. The entity is controlled under the executive branch of the government. None of the three powers of government shall share combine power. They are always separate powers. The reason for me say that is it has no judicial power. This is a separate entity that is not a part of the federal constitution. As well as Title-IV Act was never passed as law. I would like to take my name of the contract that you call a birth certificate. I didn't not agree to take a debt when I signed the affidavit for a record of birth on my daughter.

It is fraud and I can prove you have committed this vicious act. You have violated the constitution and have violated my constitutional rights. I was never aware of any legal consequences if I signed. I was never told verbally by a nurse at Barnes Jewish hospital or was it in writing stating that on the affidavit. It doesn't say I will get my wages taken, taxes garnished, license revoked, even possible incarceration for not paying. I was never aware of these consequences. So, I wasn't fully aware of what I was signing.

SEC. 466. [42 U.S.C. 666] (A) any refund of State income tax which would otherwise be payable to a noncustodial parent will be reduced, after notice has been sent to that noncustodial parent of the proposed reduction and the procedures to be followed to contest it (and after full compliance with all procedural due process requirements of the State), by the amount of any overdue support owed by such noncustodial parent;

(iii) CONTEST.—Procedures under which, after the 60-day period referred to in clause (ii), a signed voluntary acknowledgment of paternity may be challenged in court only on the *basis of fraud*, duress, or material mistake of fact, with the burden of proof upon the challenger, and under which the legal responsibilities (including child support obligations) of any signatory arising from the acknowledgment may not be suspended during the challenge, except for good cause shown.

I was stripped of my chance of due process which is where you have committed fraud twice. Once with the state of your sheriff officer written documentation saying he served paperwork to my brother. The second is depriving me of due process. Also, my chance to fight the accusations brought on my name. For the two reason above is why I would like to take my name of the contract/promissory agreement that we supposed to have amongst each other. The federal government have contracts with the state; who has contracts with the counties for collecting the funds.

The Supreme Court case of Blessing vs. Freestone 520 U.S 329(1997) states," Title IV-D does not give individuals a federal right to force a state agency to substantially comply with Title IV-D. Pp.340-349." This system called child support isn't in the best interest of our children. It's for the state to receive funds from the federal government.

"The administrative child support process governed by Minn. Stat.
518.5511 (1996) is unconstitutional because it violates the separation
of powers required by Minn. Const. art. III, 1."
(STATE OF MINNESOTA
IN COURT OF APPEALS C7-97-926 C8-97-1132 C7-97-1512 C8-98-33, Filed
June 12, 1998;

I am giving this corporation *10 days* to respond to this letter in regards of the contract which is the birth certificate to have my signature removed due to fraud and duress. If the claim for removal is denied there will be a civil case for fraud and duress on this entity called Family Support Division and the City of St. Louis, MO. As well as judges, clerks, city council etc. because it is in the judges and State best interest to keep my on-child support. Knowing that this form of payment and many more goes to the State Treasury and that's how the state officials get paid.

Sincerely, **Devion Glass 02/21/2019**

UCC1-308 without prejudice

Glossary

ENTITY- A real being; existence. Department of Banking v. Hedges, 136 Neb. 382, 286 N.W. 277,281.

CONTRACT- A promissory agreement between two or more persons that creates, modifies, or destroys a legal relation. Buffalo Pressed Steel Co. v. Kirwan, 138 Md. 60, 113 A. 628, 630; Mexican Petroleum Corporation of Louisiana v. North German Lloyd, D.C. La., 17 F.2d 113, 114.

DUE PROCESS OF LAW-Law in its regular courte of administration through courts of justice. 3 Story, Const. 264, 661. "Due process of law in each particular case means such an exercise of the powers of the government as the settled maxims of law permit and sanction, and under such safeguards for the protection of individual rights as those maxims prescribe for the class of cases to which the one in question belongs." Cooley, Const. Lim. 441.

DUE TO- Expressions "sustained by," "due to," "resulting from," "sustained by means of," "sustained in consequence 4" and "sustained through" have been held to be synonymous. Federal Life Ins. Co. v. White, Tex., 23 S.W.2d 832, 834. Also, synonymous with "caused by." American Stores Co. v. Herman, 166 Md. 312, 171 A. 54, 58.

DUE PROOF- Within policies requirements mean such a statement of facts, reasonably verified, as, if established in court, would prima facie require payment of the claim, and does not mean some particular form of proof which the insurer arbitrarily demands. Misskelley v. Home Life Ins. Co., 205 N.C. 496, 171 S.E. 862, 868; National Life Ins. Co. v. White, D.C. Mun. App., 38 A. 2d 663, 666.

EMINENT DOMAIN- The power to take private property for public use. MacVeagh v. Multonomah County, 126 Or. 417, 270 P.

RESPONSIBLE GOV.- This term generally designates that species of governmental system in which the responsibility for public measures or acts of state rests upon the ministry or executive council, who are under an obligation to resign when disapprobation of their course is expressed by a vote of want of confidence, in the legislative assembly, or by the defeat of an important measure advocated by them.

PROVISION- Foresight of the chance of an event happening, sufficient to indicate that any present undertaking upon which its assumed realization might exert a natural and proper influence was entered upon in full contemplation of it as a future possibility. Appeal of Blake, 95 Conn. 194, 110 A. 833, 834.

In English history. A name given to certain statutes or acts of parliament, particularly those intended to curb the arbitrary or usurped power of the sovereign, and also to certain other ordinances or declarations having the force of law. See infra.

References

The 42 U.S.C. §654(3) And The 45 CFR §302.34

https://www.ssa.gov/OP_Home/ssact/title04/0454.htm#

https://www.ssa.gov/OP_Home/ssact/title04/0466.htm

https://law.justia.com/cases/federal/district-courts/FSupp/789/273/1641678/

https://www.fathermag.com/news/2764-child-support.shtml

http://fathersforlife.org/famlaw/csusgeorgia.htm

https://supreme.justia.com/cases/federal/us/436/658/

https://supreme.justia.com/cases/federal/us/536/129/

https://www.govinfo.gov/content/pkg/GPO-CPRT-108WPRT108-6/pdf/GPO-CPRT-108WPRT108-6-2-8.pdf

https://www.acf.hhs.gov/sites/default/files/ocse/dcl_09_11a.pdf

https://www.acf.hhs.gov/sites/default/files/programs/css/child_support_glossary.pdf

https://www.njcourts.gov/courts/assets/family/cshopopsman20090326withattach.pdf

https://archive.org/stream/atreatiseonlawc00storgoog#page/n18/mode/2up

Library of Congress

Black Law Dictionary

For the people who don't like reading. I also put it in the music we create.

The way we live isn't the way the universe designed it to be. The hate that you hold isn't yours.

Peace Be to All- El Shaaddi

Stop Giving Your Energy Away INC.

The Negros In North America

The Illuminati

The Break Down of Religion 1, 2, & 3

The Over Turn of The Republic

Shadow Government

How to Trace Your Nationality?

What Is the Matrix 1 & 2

Who Controls the United States Corporation?

The Truth About the History of The Planet 1-4 series

Stop Giving Your Energy Away